P-51 MUSTANG
Nose Art *Gallery*

John M. and Donna Campbell

Motorbooks International
Publishers & Wholesalers ®

First published in 1994 by Motorbooks International Publishers & Wholesalers, PO Box 2, 729 Prospect Avenue, Osceola, WI 54020 USA

Motorbooks International books are also available at discounts in bulk quantity for industrial or sales-promotional use. For details write to Special Sales Manager at the Publisher's address

Library of Congress Cataloging-in-Publication Data

Campbell, John M.
    P–51 Mustang nose art gallery /John M. Campbell, Donna Campbell.
       p.   cm.
    Includes index.
    ISBN 0-87938-782-3
    1. Mustang (Fighter planes) 2. Airplanes, Military–United States–Decoration. 3. World War, 1939-1945–Aerial operations, American. I. Campbell, Donna.
II. Title.
UG1242.F5C357   1994
358.4'383–dc20   93-37242

On the front cover: A belligerent Donald Duck on the nose of a restored Mustang at the Oshkosh Air Show.

On the back cover: The Mustangs *Blue Devil, Helen, Scream'n Demon,* and *Shady Lady.*

Printed and bound in Hong Kong

Contents

Acknowledgments

We owe many people thanks for their assistance and want all of them to know that without their support and assistance this brief on the P-51 would not have been possible. Among these are Jack Ilfrey of the 20th FG; Charles G. Worman; Wesley Henry; Joseph Ventolo of Wright-Patterson AFB Museum staff; James Crowder, Ph.D.; Lura M. Casey; Don Klinko, Ph.D., of the Tinker AFB Office of History; Oklahoma Air Space Museum Director Don Finch and his executive assistant Stewart Howard; Joseph Kuhn; Maj. S. D. Huff; Jack T. Curtis; Frank and Frieda Sanders; William Fowkes; Ed Haskamp; Merle C. Olmstead; Ed Bollen; James V. Crow; Wayne Donnie Watts; Wayne Walrond; Mike and Sharon Conners of the Hobby Shop for their support and interest; Lt. Ron and Delores Willis; Thomas and Suzanne Charmichael for their enthusiasm; Jeffrey L. Ethell; Paul Fornet; J. W. Reynolds; Bill Overstreet; R. E. Casteel; E. E. Burger; Stu Ostler of Deja Vu Inc.; Ralph P. Willet; J. A. Roberts; Jack Harris; Robert Hernandez; Garry and Barbara Pape; Mike and Linda Hill; Sgt. Mark Bacon; John Stanaway; Jim Sullivan; R. Baggett; Gary James; Tom Ivey; Bill Hess; Ernie McDowell; Steve Furguson; Richard and Kathy Long; Jesse and Jewell Easton for their love and continued support during the harder trials and tribulations of the past few months; and most especially Fay D. and Ruth Campbell, my parents, for all of their tolerance, assistance, patience, and support during all these projects.

Introduction

Many men have learned of the performance of the P-51 Mustang. From the ice- and flak-filled skies of Europe to the dust-swept landing strips of the Pacific, the P-51 literally carved its reputation into the hearts and minds of all who came to recognize it.

The P-51 was revered by its pilots and ground crews. Easy to service and a "princess" to fly, many an ace would be made at the controls of the hearty Mustang. The crewmen would name the airplane in many instances for the pilot or his wife or girlfriend, and in some cases, for their distinct hatred for an enemy of a war now nearly fifty years past.

The P-51 was soon respected by all the airmen who had the misfortune to fall victim to her powerful guns. And in peacetime the P-51 has been a much sought-after treasure to fly, to own, to race in. Air racers now seek this stallion in hopes of fulfilling dreams of racing victories.

Whether you see the Mustang at your favorite air show or flew it in combat, you'll remember the colorful names and slogans still adorning a few examples that still remain. We hope you will all enjoy this brief and perhaps reflect back on the days of valor and high adventure.

Nose Art Gallery

Shady Lady, a P-51 of the 67th Tactical Reconnaissance Squadron (TRS), was adorned with a young lady wearing only silk stockings and high heels.

OKaye was piloted by LeLand "Tommy" Molland. A former spitfire pilot, Molland was credited with 10.5 victories in WWII. He was later killed in the Korean War.

Lt. Col. Charles Boedeker, assigned to the 52nd Fighter Group (FG), piloted the P-51 named *Doris Faye II*.

O'Sage Chief (s/n 44-13855) was piloted by Capt. Harold Binkley.

This P-51 named *Little Rock III* flew in the China-Burma-India (CBI) theater. The pilot was Charles Glanville.

Bobby Jeanne flew with the 357th FG in World War II.

Papp's Answer was piloted by Lt. Robert Smith of the 357th FG. Smith was killed in action (KIA).

Gentle Annie was piloted by Col. Harold Rau. This aircraft belonged to the 20th FG, stationed at Kingscliffe, England.

Hurry Home Honey, a P-51D (s/n 44-14868) piloted by Capt. Richard Peterson assigned to the 364th Fighter Squadron (FS), 357th FG.

Round Trip Jr. was a P-51 assigned to the 357th FG.

Lt. Frank Bouldin of the 352nd FS, 353rd FG, piloted *Dallas Doll* (s/n 44-14495).

Patty IV, a P-51D (s/n 44-13983) assigned to the 352nd FG, shows three kill marks.

1st Lt. Edward Bollen piloted *Eadie Mae.* Bollen was assigned to the 75th FS, 23rd FG, in the CBI.

The P-51 named *Lope's Hope 3rd*, was piloted by 1st Lt. Donald Lopez who was assigned to the 75th FS, 23rd FG.

Left to right, Lt. Bill Davenport, Lt. John Ellis, Jr., and Lt. Lefe Bure are seen on *Pride of The Blue Grass*, an F-6, assigned to the 12th Photo Reconnaissance Squadron (PRS). *Davenport via Ivey*

The P-51, *American Beauty*, was piloted by John James Voll of the 308th FS, 31st FG, who was credited with 21 victories in the MTO.

Flying Dutchman was flown by Lt. Robert Goebel, 308th FS, Mediterranean Theater of Operations (MTO).

Avery was the name carried by this P-51D assigned to the 342nd FS, 348th FG. This photo was taken on a field in the Southwest Pacific after Avery crash landed.

Lt. Col. Robert Richard Rowland piloted *Dirty Dick IV*. Rowland flew with the 348th FG, where he was credited with 8 aerial victories, all in the P-47. Rowland was the executive officer to Neal Kearby and took over as group commander upon Kearby's transfer to V Fighter Command.

This P-51D, named *Major Astired*, belonged to the 82nd TRS.

Ida/Lady Lynn/Vern, a P-51D, belonged to the 82nd TRS.

Col. William Banks, commanding officer (CO) of the 348th FG, flew *Sunshine VII* (s/n 44-12073). Standing with Banks is "Doc" Alston, crew chief (c/c) of the colonel's aircraft.

Seen here is *Lil' Onie*, a P-51D assigned to the 82nd TRS, on assignment to the 348th FG, Ie Shima.

The P-51D *Bootsie* belonged to the 341st FS, 348th FG, Ie Shima.

Lacka Nookie, a P-51D, belonged to the 82nd TRS, assigned to the 348th FG, Ie Shima.

Lt. Schlegel of the 341st FS piloted the P-51D *Wee Willie's Wagon*. This aircraft was turned over to the 8th FG at the war's end.

The Flying Undertaker (s/n 44-72505) was the aircraft of Maj. William Shomo. Shomo was assigned to the 82nd TRS, 71st TRG. Shomo scored 8 victories and was awarded the Medal of Honor.

The P-51 *Irene Ann* belonged to the 342nd FS, 348th FG.

Beef Injection was one of the P-51s assigned to the 342nd FS, 348th FG.

The P-51D *We Three* (s/n 44-12822) belonged to the 110th TRS, 71st TRG.

Snooks -5th, a P-51D (s/n 44-14841) assigned to the 82nd TRS, 71st TRG, is seen with c/c Ralph Winkle. Winkle was also c/c of *The Flying Undertaker*.

This photo of the P-51 *Lorene* was taken at Le Brouget Airport in 1944.

Lady Marion (s/n 44-64113) was piloted by Lt. K. W. Greever, belonged to the 342nd FS, 348th FG, Ie Shima, August 1945.

The CO of the 460th FS, Capt. William Dunham, flew the P-51D *Mrs. Bonnie*. Dunham has 16 victories to his credit, but only one was in a Mustang.

Members of the 348th FG are pictured with the P-51Ds *Rotation Blues* and *Pretty Betty* on Ie Shima, 1945.

Miss Jeanie (s/n 44-12033) was assigned to the 340th FS, 348th FG, and is pictured on Ie Shima.

Lady Marion (s/n 44-64113) was assigned to the 342nd FS, 348th FG, and is pictured on Ie Shima, August 1945.

This 59th FG P-51 was named *Tojo-Peach*.

This P-51D was assigned to Lt. Col. Robert Rowland of the 348th FG.

The P-51D (s/n 44-14153) *Cooter* is flying in this formation of 357th FG aircraft.

The P-51B *Joan* belonged to the 357th FG.

Lt. Robert Powell, Jr., piloted the P-51 (s/n 42-106914) named *The West by Gawd Virginian*.

Lieutenant Childers piloted the F-6C *Oh Johnie* (s/n 43-25081).

The palm tree in this art forms the "T" in the name *Tampa Joe*. These bathing beauties were on the F-6 assigned to Leo Elliott who was assigned to the 12th RS.

Rosalie was piloted by Lt. Joshua "Chief" Sanford and maintained by T/Sgt. Myron Funmaker, both Native Americans. This P-51 was assigned to the 75th FS, 23rd FG.

Lt. Edward Kenny III piloted the F-6C *Shovelnose and Handlebar* (s/n 42-103613) with the 162nd TRS, 10th PRG, 9th Air Force (AF).

15

This P-51D, assigned to the 75th FS, 23rd FG, was named *Hillzapoppin* after its pilot, Meredith Hill. The 23rd FG was stationed in the CBI.

The P-51 *Cornhusker* also has a Native American flare.

The Iron Chit Bird was the name on this P-51D (s/n 44-64220).

Lt. B. W. Scott piloted this RF-51K, *Tulie, Scotty & ?*, assigned to the 45th TRS.

Mazie, Me and Monk was an F-6 of the 12th TRS. It was named for c/c Monk Davidson, the pilot, Capt. "Blackie" Travis (me), and a lady named Mazie.

1st Lt. Jesse Gray piloted *The Streak*. Gray was assigned to the 75th FS, 23rd FG.

Little Que (s/n 44-72606) was assigned to the 458th FS, 506th FG, Iwo Jima. The aircraft was piloted by Lt. Q. Lee.

2nd Lt. Gordon Willis piloted *Alta Marie That's my baby*. Willis was assigned to the 75th FS, 23rd FG.

These men, assigned to the 352nd FG, are jokingly boring a hole in the tire on the P-51D *Katydid*.

This Mustang wears the name *Tottie*.

The P-51D *Gloria Ann 2nd* is pictured at Site A-89, Belgium, in the winter of 1944 or 1945.

This P-51 was named *Abdul*.

This young lady was on the P-51D *Deviless 3rd*.

18

The crew poses with this P-51 named *Pride of the Yanks*.

The crew work on the 357th FG P-51D named *Alice Marie II*.

A P-51D named *Jack of Hearts IV*.

This shark mouth was on the *Vivacious Virgin III*, piloted by 1st Lt. I. B. MacKenzie.

The P-51D *Satan's Flame* had a very small piece of art on its nose and the name *Maggie*.

The P-51 *Old Glory* shows the American flag flying proudly.

The P-51D *Madam Wham-Dam* was assigned to the 458th FS, 506th FG, and is shown parked at-the-ready at North Field, Iwo Jima 1945.

This P-51D was named *Nancy June 3rd*.

This Varga calendar girl art on a P-51 was accompanied by the name *Lady Joan III*.

Maj. George Preddy piloted the P-51D *Cripes A'Mighty 3rd*. Preddy was assigned to the 487th FS, 352nd FG.

The crew poses with the P-51 named *Queenie II*.

A pilot wearing his flying gear stands on the P-51D *Rattop IV*.

The pilot sits on the wing of his P-51D named *Swanee Jr.*

Capt. William Whisner piloted the P-51 *Princess Elizabeth* (s/n 42-106449) assigned to the 487th FS, 352nd FG.

The P-51D *Happy Jr* (s/n 44-14731) carries 7 victory marks.

Straw Boss 2 (s/n 44-14111) was piloted by Col. James Mayden, CO of the 352nd FG.

Maj. Jack Ilfrey piloted the P-51D *Happy Jack's Go Buggy* (s/n 44-13761). Ilfrey was the CO of the 79th FS, 20th FG.

The P-51D *Sweet Thing IV* carries 8 victory marks.

These crew members pose with the P-51 named *Heat Wave*.

Col. Everett Stewart, CO of the 4th FG, piloted the P-51D named *Sunny VIII*.

The F-6 named *Rex*, belonged to Lieutenant Vesley of the 161st TRS, 363rd TRG.

Capt. Don Gentile, assigned to the 336th FS, 4th FG, piloted the P-51, *Shangri-La* (s/n 43-6913).

My Kath was a P-51 assigned to the 20th FG.

Col. Joe Mason of the 486th FS, 352nd FG, piloted the P-51D *This Is It!* (s/n 42-106609).

The P-51D *Patty Ann II* (s/n 42-108872) of the 328th FS, 352nd FG, came in on its belly.

Taking off is the P-51D named *Deuces Wild*. This aircraft belonged to the 356th FS, 354th FG.

Ready for takeoff is the P-51D *Miss Wabbit IV*.

This is another P-51 named *Heat Wave*. This one has flames coming from the letters to add to the effect.

Col. Thomas Christian piloted the P-51D *Lou IV*
(s/n 44-13410), assigned to the 375th FS, 361st FG.

The P-51D (s/n 44-14251) *Contrary Mary* belonged to the
84th FS, 78th FG.

This young lady was painted on the P-51 named *Spare Parts*.

Capt. Gerald Fine piloted the P-51D named *Jeanne II* (s/n 44-15493), assigned to the 385th FS.

This P-51D of the 20th FG was named *Claudine I*.

Capt. Andrew Turner, CO of the 100th FS, 332nd FG, piloted the P-51 *Skipper's Darlin'*.

The P-51 *Virgins All* was piloted by William Thomas who flew in both World War II and Korea.

The damage to the P-51 *Sally* was inflicted when the aircraft flew in too low on a strafing mission over a German airfield.

The P-51 *Starck Mad!* belonged to the 352nd FG, stationed at Bodney, England.

Lil' Aggie was the name on this P-51 belonging to the 352nd FG, Bodney, England.

The P-51 *Peanuts* belonged to the 352nd FG.

Gig's Up II was piloted by Major Gignac who flew with the 486th FS, 352nd FG.

The P-51 *Nancy M.* of the 352nd FG.

The men celebrate the art on the P-51 *Miss E.T.O.* by posing with the young lady whose likeness appears on the aircraft.

The P-51 named *Miss Lace* belonged to the 486th FS, 352nd FG.

The P-51 *It's Supermouse* belonged to the 328th FS, 352nd FG.

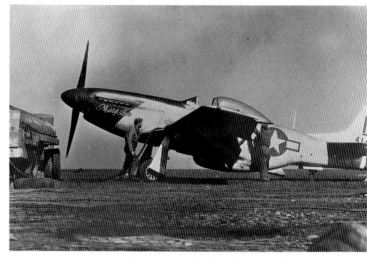

The P-51D *Mary Lou* belonged to the 352nd FG.

Colonel Duncan of the 353rd FG piloted the P-51 *Dove of Peace*.

Lil Evey III suffered a bad landing. This aircraft belonged to the 352nd FG.

Maj. Lowell Brueland piloted the P-51 *Grim Reaper*. Brueland was assigned to the 355th FS, 354th FG.

1st Lt. Sheldon Heyer of the 487th FS, 352nd FG, piloted the
P-51 *Sweetie Face*.

Uno-Who? was piloted by Maj. George Lamb of the 356th
FS, 354th FG.

Lt. Col. Richard Turner piloted the P-51D *Short-Fuse* when
he flew with the 356th FS, 354th FG.

This P-51D was flown by Maj. Glenn Eagleston of the 353rd FS, 354th FG. Eagleston scored 18.5 confirmed aerial victories.

The P-51B named *Killer* was piloted by Maj. Robert Stephens of the 355th FS, 354th FG.

Col. James Howard piloted *Ding Hao*. This aircraft belonged to the 356th FS, 354th FG.

1st Lt. Glenn Crum piloted the P-51D *Koyli Renee*. This aircraft belonged to the 359th FS, 356th FG.

The P-51D *Nazi Hot Foot* of the 359th FS, 356th FG.

The P-51D *Starduster* was assigned to the 359th FS, 356th FG.

Ole-II (s/n 43-6928) was piloted by Maj. William J. Hovde of the 355th FG, who was credited with 12.5 aerial victories.

Killer! was piloted by Maj. Robert Stephens of the 355th FS, 354th FG. Stephens was credited with 13 aerial victories.

This dragon was the insignia of the 357th FS, 355th FG. Seen with the aircraft is the squadron CO Maj. John Elder (right) and his c/c, Billy Mitchell. Major Elder scored 8 aerial victories and damaged one.

Little Shrimp (s/n 463621) was piloted by Maj. Robert W. Foy of the 363rd FS, 357th FG, who was credited with 15 aerial victories.

Jane VII (s/n 44-72953) was assigned to Maj. Bert W. Marshall, Jr., of the 354th FS, 355th FG, who was credited with 7 aerial victories.

Texas Terror IV (s/n 44-13571), assigned to the 354th FS, 355th FG, was piloted by Lt. Lee G. Mendenhall who was credited with 0.5 aerial victories.

U've Had It! (s/n 42-106452) was piloted by Maj. John B. England, assigned to the 362nd FS, 357th FG. Major England had 17.5 aerial victories.

Nooky Booky IV (s/n 44-11622) was piloted by Maj. Leonard "Kit" Carson of the 362nd FS, 357th FG. Carson is credited with 18.5 aerial victories.

Passion Wagon, was piloted by Lt. Arval J. Roberson, assigned to the 362nd FS, 357th FG. Roberson is credited with 6 aerial victories.

Desert Rat (s/n 44-13714) was piloted by Lt. Hershel T. Pascoe of the 363rd FS, 357th FG. Pascoe is credited with 1 aerial victory.

This P-51D (s/n 44-72199) was piloted by Capt. Charles E. Weaver of the 362nd FS, 357th FG. Frank Hurbis is pictured with the aircraft.

Berlin Express (s/n 42-103309) was piloted by Lt. William B. Overstreet of the 363rd FS, 357th FG. Overstreet is credited with 2.25 aerial victories.

Shoo Shoo Baby (s/n 42-106447) belonged to the 364th FS, 357th FG.

This later *Berlin Express* was also the ride of Lt. William B. Overstreet.

This view of Lt. William B. Overstreet's P-51D *Berlin Express* shows the winged horse painted on the starboard side.

Shanty Irish was piloted by Lt. Gilbert Mouzon O'Brien of the 362nd FS, 357th FG. O'Brien is credited with 7 aerial victories and 2.5 aircraft damaged.

The P-51C *Big Mac Junior* was piloted by Capt. John R. Brown of the 364th FS, 357th FG. Brown damaged an FW 190 on 12 July 1944 while at the controls of this aircraft.

The P-51C *$Blackpool Bat* (s/n 43-24842) was piloted by George G. George of the 363rd FS, 357th FG.

Glamorous Glen III (s/n 44-14888) was piloted by Capt. Charles E. "Chuck" Yeager of the 363rd FS, 357th FG.

Louisiana Heat Wave, was piloted by Lieutenant Crenshaw of the 369th FS, 357th FG. Crenshaw has 7 aerial victories.

Lonesome Polecat (s/n 44-14356) was piloted by Lt. Keehn Landis of the 363rd FS, 357th FG. Landis has 1 victory earned on 18 September 1944.

Mountaineer was piloted by Lt. Paul N. Bowles of the 363rd FS, 357th FG. Bowles downed an Me-262 jet fighter on 19 April 1945.

Marymae belonged to the 362nd FS, 357th FG.

Moose (s/n 44-63221) was piloted by Lt. M. A. "Moose" Beacraft of the 362nd FS, 357th FG.

Pilot George G. George is seen sitting on the wing of the P-51 *$Blackpool Bat* with his future wife who was from Blackpool.

Little Joe (s/n 44-13887) was piloted by Lt. Joe Cannon of the 363rd FS, 357th FG. Cannon damaged an Me-262 on 19 March 1945.

Horses Itch (s/n 44-13518) was piloted by Maj. Edwin W. Hiro of the 363rd FS, 357th FG. Hiro is credited with 5 aerial victories.

Ferocious Frankie was piloted by Lt. Col. Wallace E. Hopkins of the 361st FG. Hopkins had 4 aerial victories.

Texas Ranger (s/n 43-6698) was piloted by Lt. Otto D. Jenkins of the 362nd FS, 357th FG, who scored 8.5 aerial victories.

City of Paris was piloted by Maj. Robert McWherter of the 382nd FS, 363rd FG. McWherter scored 4 aerial victories.

Nancy Lee was assigned to the 402nd FS, 370th FG.

Cassies Chassie was piloted by Lt. Manuel L. Casagrande of the 383rd FS, 364th FG.

Princess Marge was piloted by Lt. Raymond E. Schillenef of the 382nd FS, 363rd FG. Lieutenant Schillenef shot down an FW 190 on 12 July 1944.

Jeanne II was piloted by Capt. Gerald Fine of the 385th FS, 364th FG.

41

Gross Arsch Vogel was assigned to the 385th FS, 364th FG, as seen here at Honnington, England.

Pictured with the P-51 *Smoky Joe* are Lt. Valentine Rizzo (left), athletic officer, and Lt. Joe Gerst, both of whom lived on the same block in the smoky city of Pittsburgh.

The P-51 *Punkin II* was piloted by Lt. Robert S. Faulkner of the 384th FS, 364th FG.

The P-51 *Fran 2nd* of the 350th FS, 353rd FG.

The pilot and crew are seen here with the P-51 *T-Lou-II*.

The P-51 *Patricia Jean* is pictured during takeoff.

A pilot poses with his P-51D *Lil Curley*.

Pilots and crew pose with the P-51 *My Norma*.

The P-51D *Sebastian Jr.* belonged to the 357th FG.

Nevada Skat Kat belonged to the 357th FG.

The P-51D *Is This Trip Necessary?* belonged to the 506th FG.

An aerial view of the P-51D *Silver Streak*.

The P-51D *Flying Dutchman* belonged to the 356th FG.

A small Indian maid was on this P-51 assigned to the 359th BG.

This art was on a P-51 assigned to the 363rd Bomb Group (BG).

Maj. Donald Bochkay piloted the P-51 *Speedball Alice*, which belonged to the 357th FG.

The P-51D *Ann Anita/Alabama Bound* belonged to the 355th BG.

The P-51D *Dragon Wagon* belonged to the 355th BG.

The P-51D *Beautiful Betty* belonged to the 352nd FG.

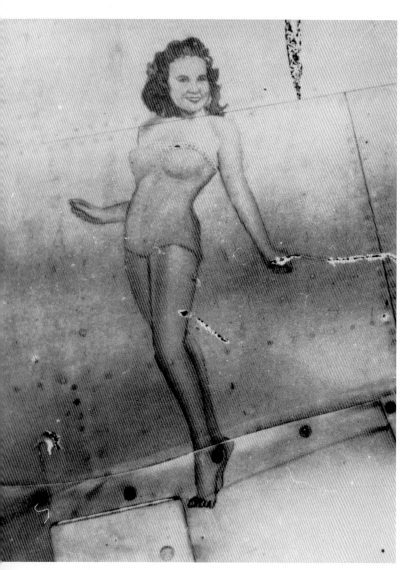

Unnamed P-51 art.

This airborne P-51D was named *Philly-Dillies*.

The wind and sand were on the mind of the artist who painted the art on *Desert Rat*.

Miss Margie Sue, Rebel Gal (s/n 44-15417) was assigned to the 2nd Air Commando Group.

Capt. Richard Peterson of the 364th FS, 357th FG, piloted *Hurry Home Honey* (s/n 44-13586).

The P-51D *Tika IV* (s/n 44-13357) was assigned to the 374th FS, 361st FG.

The P-51D *Marilyn's Marauder* of the 356th FG.

The P-51D *Man O'War* (s/n 44-73144) belonged to the 354th FS, 355th FG.

This P-51C was assigned to the 23rd FG in World War II. The early Mustang is believed to be that of Col. Tex Hill (who had also flown with the Flying Tigers) in the China Burma India Theater of Operations.

Captain McDonald, with the 12th FIS, piloted this Mustang named *Doris-II/Swing Lo.*

Chappie James, who eventually became a four-star general, stands by his Mustang showing a shark-mouth design. James served during World War II with the Tuskegee Airmen. He also served with the 12th FIS in Korea, where this photo was taken.

These Mustangs, assigned to the 12th FIS, are lined up at
K-10 airfield, Korea.

Jazz Baby (FF-920) was the first of five Mustangs to be flown
by Lt. Robert S. Fogg. This photo was taken in April 1949
while the aircraft was assigned to the 95th FIS.

Bad Check–Always Comes Back is seen here at K-2 airfield,
Korea, in September 1950.

Ole Mission Minnie was assigned to the 35th FIS in September 1950.

Harry Peyser is in the cockpit of his F-51D while based at Grenier AFB in 1949. The 113th FIS insignia is visible on the right-hand side of his aircraft.

Pictured is *Jazz Baby IV* after the last F-51 mission of the Korean War, December 1950. The pilot, Bob Fogg, is standing with his aircraft at K-16 airfield, Korea.

Buckeye Blitz VI/Mac's Revenge was piloted by Maj. William O'Donnell, commander of the 36th FIS, which was nicknamed the Flying Fiends.

Oh-Kaye Baby, RF-51D assigned to the 45th TRS at Kimpo, Korea. In the United States this aircraft was in the Air National Guard based at Will Rogers in Oklahoma City.

Ol'Anchor Ass, an F-51 assigned to the 36th FIS, was flown by Maj. William J. O'Donnell, commander of the 36th FIS.

The P-51, *Kitten*, was piloted by Capt. Charles E. McGee of the 302nd FS, 332nd FG, during the Korea War. McGee was credited during World War II with one FW 190 on 24 August 1944.

Tulie, Scotty & ?, an RF-51K assigned to the 45th TRS, was piloted by B. W. Scott. This photo was taken at K-47 Chin Chan, Korea, 1952.

Many squadrons would adorn their aircraft in a paint scheme that would clearly identify the aircraft assigned to their squadron. This Mustang was assigned to the 57th FG at Luke AFB.

Minuteman (s/n 44-73656), assigned to the Texas Air National Guard, wears the tail banding and state outline still in use today on Texas ANG.

Today the Mustangs owned by a lucky few still show the evidence of the artist's brush. This beautiful restoration,

Passion Wagon, piloted by George Enhohning is representative of one owner's love for his machine.

Red Baron, a highly modified Mustang, was sponsored by Anheuser-Busch and Michelob beer. This aircraft was destroyed in an emergency landing at the Reno air races.

This P-51D, beautifully restored to military configuration, shows the markings of Lt. M. A. "Moose" Beacraft of the 362nd FS, 357th FG.

Shangri-La, a restored P-51C, is painted in the markings of Capt. Don S. "Buckeye" Gentile of the 336th FS, 4th FG.

Gentile is credited with 21.84 aerial victories. He survived the war but was later killed in an aircraft accident.

This P-51D was named *Little Chic*.

This P-51D art asked the big question, *Willit Run?* This aircraft belonged to the 353rd FG.

1st Lt. Sheldon Heyer of the 487th FS, 352nd FG, piloted the P-51D *Sweetie Face*.

Lt. B. Mayer of the 2nd Air Commando Group piloted the P-51D *Cheese Cake Chassis* in the CBI, 1945.

This shot of Lt. Col. John C. Meyer's P-51D shows his victory credits and the art known as *Petie*.

Capt. Kirke Everson of the 504th FS, 339th FG, piloted the P-51D *Tar Heel*.

Capt. Don Gentile of the 336th FS, 4th FG, piloted the P-51 *Shangri-La* (s/n 43-6913).

The P-51 *Mrs. Virginia* flew with the 1st Air Commando Group. It is seen flying over Burma.

Maj. Pierce McKennon of the 335th FS, 4th FG, piloted *Ridge Runner III* (s/n 44-14221).

A later version of *Shangri La*.

Lt. Sherman Childers piloted the F-6C *Oh Johnie* (s/n 43-25081) of the 109th TRS.

The RF-51 *Betty Jane* was assigned to the 45th TRS.

1st Lt. Bill Walterman of the 75th FS, 23rd FG, piloted the P-51 *Little Nell*.

Three cartoon characters on the fuselage of this P-51 of the 67th Fighter-Bomber Squadron (FBS), 18th Fighter-Bomber Wing (FBW), Korean War.

Joe Summey piloted the P-51 *Patricia*. Summery was assigned to the 75th FS 23rd FG.

1st Lt. Russ Fleming of the 75th FS, 23rd FG, piloted the P-51 *Dakota Maid*.

A pair of dice and a poker hand decorated the nose of the P-51 *Monaleone*, assigned to the 27th FG.

The P-51 *Miss Kitty/Rosie the Red Devil* was piloted by Lt. John "Rosie" Rosenbaum.

The P-51D *Gracie II* belonged to the 75th FS, 23rd FG.

2nd Lt. Joe Blackburn of the 5th FS, 52nd FG, piloted the P-51D *Little Joe* (s/n 43-24818).

1st Lt. Stanley Pell of the 4th FS, 52nd FG, piloted the P-51 *Lady Jane II*.

1st Lt. Bruno Dangelmaier of the 2nd FS, 52nd FG, piloted the P-51D *Scotty III*.

Lt. Col. Charles Boedeker of the 5th FS, 52nd FG, piloted the P-51 *Doris-Faye*.

Capt. John Clarke, Jr., of the 2nd FS, 52nd FG, piloted the P-51D *Dottie*.

A reclining lady on the nose of the P-51D *Tennessee Belle*.

This aerial view is of the P-51D *Lucky Wabbit II*, assigned to the 343th FS, 55th FG.

The P-51D *Patricia Dean* belonged to the 39th FG.

The P-51D *Kiss-Me* belonged to the 35th FG.

The P-51K *Annette* belonged to the 38th FS, 55th FG.

This P-51D was named *Beautiful Doll*.

The P-51D (s/n 44-63620) *Small Boy Here* after a landing accident. This aircraft belonged to the 78th FG.

This shark-mouth P-51D (s/n 44-74801) is seen with Capt. Howard "Ebe" Ebersole of the 18th FBG, Korea.

The P-51D *Missouri Armada* belonged to Colonel Edwards of the 357th FG. Left to right, Lt. "Dittie" Jenkins (KIA), Col. John England, Capt. Alva Murphy (KIA), and "Kit" Carson.

The P-51D *Minuteman* belonged to the Texas Air National Guard (ANG).

The P-51D *Yankees'* belonged to the 363rd FS, 357th FG.

Man-O-War (s/n 41-1683) was piloted by Capt. Kenneth E. Hagen of the 362nd FS, 357th FG.

The P-51D *Miss Velma* belonged to the 343rd FS, 55th FG.

Draggin' Seeds was piloted by Lt. Robert W. Blandin of the 402nd FS, 370th FG.

Left to right are Lieutenant Lanque, Major Boone, Lieutenant Lee, Lieutenant Agnew and Lieutenant Colonel Bailey of the 350th FS, 353rd FG, with the P-51 *Double Trouble Two*.

Salem Representative (s/n 42-106924) was piloted by Ralph "Kid" Hoffer of the 334th FS, 4th FG.

What's Up Doc!, unknown squadron and group, Eighth Air Force.

The P-51 *Wichita Warrior II* was assigned to the 350th FS, 353rd FG.

Big Stud, a P-51 (s/n 41-4819), was assigned to the 362nd FS, 357th FG, and piloted by J. L. Robinson.

The P-51 *Alabama Rammer Jammer* was piloted by
Lt. Arthur C. Cundy of the 352nd FS, 353rd FG.

Windy City was assigned to the 83rd FS, 78th FG.

Maximum Barney, a P-51 (s/n 44-72768), was assigned to the
402nd FS, 370th FG.

The P-51 *Davy Don Chariot* belonged to 353rd FG. Seen here
in a moment of leisure are the pilot and ground crew.

Texan, assigned to the 363rd FS, 357th FG, is seen with two
of the group's great aces, Bud Anderson (center) and Chuck
Yeager (far right).

Romaine (s/n 41-4792) is seen after a hard belly landing.
This aircraft was assigned to the 357th FG.

Double Trouble was the first of two Mustangs with the same name assigned to the 350th FS, 353rd FG.

The Hun Hunter/Texas, assigned to the 355th FG, was piloted by Capt. Henry Brown. Captain Brown scored 14.2 aerial victories.

Sad Sack (s/n 44-14822) was piloted by Maj. Merle J. Gilbertson of the 77th FS, 20th FG.

Double Trouble Two, a P-51D assigned to the 350th FS, 353rd FG, is seen undergoing field maintenance.

This P-51D (L-MC s/n 43-25054) landed at Lillie, France, out of gas. This aircraft was piloted by Lt. Willard H. Lewis, Jr., of the 20th FG.

In many cases nose art, or the names associated with aircraft art, is only a simple expression or a lucky talisman as seen here with the four-leaf clover for luck on the lower cowl. This P-51D was assigned to the 385th FS, 364th FG.

The Flying Mouse was piloted by Lt. James "Mouse" Carter of the 75th FS, 23rd FG.

The P-51 *Japeth IV,* assigned to the 75th FS, 23rd FG, is seen here at Chinkiang, China.

The P-51 *Anna Lee, Louisiana Lady* was piloted by Capt. Sam Dance of the 73rd FS, 23rd FG. Dance was killed in action over Hangyang.

On the P-51 *Helen* we see a little cherub with a Thompson submachine gun. This aircraft was assigned to the 4th FG.

Dirty Old Man assigned to the 460th FS, 348th FG, was piloted by Walter G. Benz, with 8 aerial victories to his credit.

This P-51D was piloted by Maj. Harry Clay Crim, Jr., of the 531st FS, 21st FG, SWPA. Note the art on the landing gear door.

Tar Heel met its fate during a night attack by the Japanese. Not too much remains of this venerable fighter.

Little remains of these two Mustangs caught on the ground during a Japanese night attack. The name on one was *Cherry*.

The P-51 *Malicious Maureen* was piloted by Kirk Kirkpatrick of 75th FS, 23rd FG.

Aircraft art has the tendency of showing up just about anywhere on an aircraft. This aircraft was assigned to the 357th FG.

The Talking Dog was piloted by Frederick Graber of the 75th FS, 23rd FG.

The P-51 *Ma Cherie* belonged to the 402nd FS, 370th FG.

The P-51 *Hot Shot Charlie* was piloted by Lt. Charles E. Nelson of the 402nd FS, 370th FG.

Little Sandy was piloted by Lt. D. R. Boyett of the 402nd FS, 370th FG.

The P-51 *My Darling Barbara IV* was piloted by Lt. James J. Ward of the 402nd FS, 370th FG.

The P-51 *Jeanne* was piloted by Lt. Joe Breckler of the 402nd FS, 370th FG.

Draggin' Seeds was piloted by Lt. Robert W. Blandin of the 402nd FS, 370th FG.

Scream'n Demon, a P-51D-20-NA (s/n 44-63207), was assigned to the 78th FG.

The P-51 *Queen of San Joaquin V* was piloted by Lt. Bert Lowe of the 402nd FS, 70th FG.

The P-51 *Mickey IV* was piloted by Lt. Elbert W. Lineker of the 402nd FS, 370th FG. Lineker is credited with 1 FW 190 destroyed.

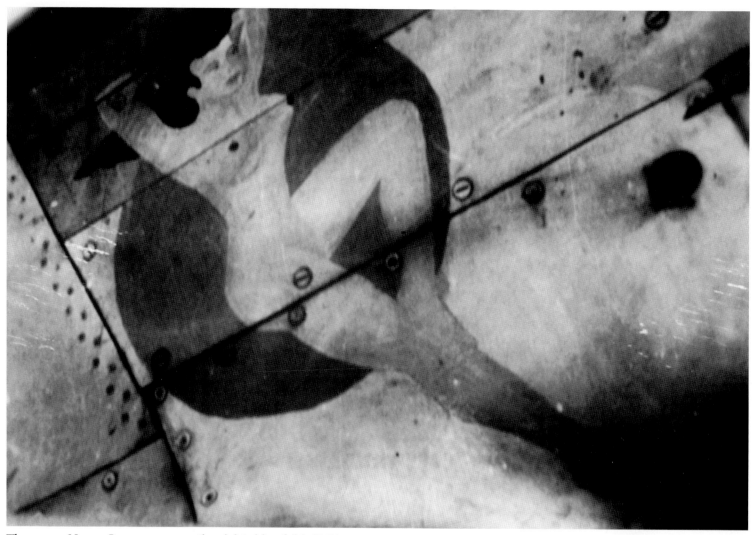

The name *Nancy Lee* appears on the right side of this P-51,
piloted by Lt. R. Baggett of the 402nd FS, 370th FG.

The P-51 *Mrs. Wabbit IV* was piloted by Lieutenant Hirsch of
the 402nd FS, 370th FG.

The P-51 *Sierra Sue II* was piloted by Lt. Robert H. Bohna of
the 402nd FS, 370th FG. Bohna shot down one FW 190.

The P-51 *Bubby Honey* was piloted by Lt. Sam Goldman of the 402nd FS, 370th FG.

The P-51 *Princess Irene, Ma Petite Cherie* belonged to the 402nd FS, 370th FG.

The P-51 *Daisy June* belonged to the 402nd FS, 370th FG.

Princess Margaret was piloted by Lt. Raymond E. Schillenef of the 382nd FS, 363rd FG. Schillenef scored one aerial victory.

Essie Mae II was assigned to the 402nd FS, 370th FG.

Old Eli was piloted by Lt. J. Leary of the 402nd FS, 370th FG.

My Baby was assigned to 402nd FS, 370th FG.

Dear Edna was assigned to the 402nd FS, 370th FG.

Lil' Sis was assigned to the 70th FS, 20th FG, based at Kingscliffe, England.

Keep Smilin' (s/n 44-63819) was assigned to the 402nd FS, 370th FG. This art is on the left-hand side of *Hot Shot Charlie*.

Tiny Gay Baba (s/n 44-63955) was assigned to the 46th FS, 21st FG.

Gash-Hound, assigned to the 402nd FS, 370th FG, shows two aerial victories and a nice canine with the raised tail in salute to the *Reich*.

Nelle Jo was assigned to the 342nd FS, 348th FG, SWPA.

Upups C pops! was assigned to the 353rd FG.

Dee & Shy Ann, with two sister ships, flies formation over southern France. This aircraft was assigned to the 503rd FS, 339th FG.

The P-51C *Miss Appropriated* was found and made flyable at Orleans-Bricy, France, by Colonel Hal of the 394th BG, Ninth Air Force. It was later turned over to 370th FG.

Tommy, an F-51D, was assigned to the 12th FBS, 18th FBW, at Chinhae (K-10) airfield, South Korea.

Little Bitch, a P-51C, was piloted by Capt. Dave T. Perron of the 362nd FS, 357th FG.

Batty Betty, rigged and geared for the air racing circuit, still carries the battlefield name and the stenciled number 34.

This P-51H, assigned to the 148th Fighter Interceptor Squadron (FIS) of the Pennsylvania ANG, has a simple example of nose art, the squadron insignia.

This post-war Mustang wears the insignia of the USAF
Training Command.

Muddy (s/n 44-11697), assigned to the 362nd FS, 357th FG,
was piloted by Lt. James A. Gasser.

Lil' Marie (s/n 41-4306) was assigned to the 31st PRS,
67th TRG.

Thunderbird, a P-51C, is shown dressed up in 1947 air-race markings.

Fat Cat is spruced up in air racing garb with number and corporate sponsor decals.

The P-51D *Floogie II* was assigned to the 357th FG.

Baby! III was piloted by Lt. J. H. Baldwin of the 70th FS, 20th FG.

Blue Devil, an F-6D of the 12th TRS, 10th TRG, was based at
RAF Ford, Chalgrove, England, in the summer of 1944.

Beguine was a highly modified P-51C raced at the Cleveland
air races.

A flight of 20th FG P-51Ds over the English countryside.
Note group's signature cowl stripes.

Strellita III was assigned to the 364th FG. The forward cowl
has blue and white stripes running horizontally, and the
canopy rail has a blue-and-white checker design.

Penny, a P-51D assigned to the 364th Fighter Group.

4 Esie, assigned to the 364th FG, sits at the ready.

Coffin Wit' Wings, this P-51D assigned to the 364th FG, shows evidence of a taxi accident.

This P-51B (s/n 43-6510) of the 363rd FS, 357th FG, crashed in a field on 18 September 1944 breaking the fuselage.

Thelma of the 364th FG also came into contact with the hard deck.

Diablo, meaning devil in Latin, was assigned to the 352nd FG, based at Bodney, England.

Lt. Richard T. Bond piloted *Bond Baby* with the 20th FG.

Hawk Jalopy was assigned to the 84th FS, 78th FG.

Nina Merle II was piloted by Lt. Merle Jones of the 77th FS, 20th FG.

Lucky Leaky II, assigned to the 352nd FS, 353rd FG, is seen here after coming to grief after a belly landing.

Li'L Daddy was a P-51D assigned to the 20th FG.

Ina, The Macon Belle was a P-51D piloted by Lt. Lee A. Archer of the 302nd FS, 332nd FG, the "Tuskeegee Airmen."

A 20th FG Mustang.

Tempe Queen was named for the city of Tempe, Arizona.

Happy, a P-51C, was assigned to the 339th Fighter Group.

This is *Ol' Nadsob*, an F-51D (s/n 45-11742) of the 67th FBS, 18th FBG.

This F-51H is seen in the markings of the District of Colombia with the nation's Capitol building embossed on the tail.

Chicago Gun Moll, a P-51B, was piloted by Lt. Robert D. Brown of the 362nd FS, 357th FS. Brown had two aerial victories.

The Shillelagh was piloted by Lt. Col. John A. Storch of the 364th FS, 357th FG. Storch scored 10.5 aerial victories.

Dakota Kid (s/n 42-103317), a P-51B, belonged to the 358th FS of the 355th FS.

Hoo Flung Dung (s/n 43-6438), C3-M, was assigned to the 382nd FS of the 363rd FG.*Dee*, a P-51D of the 339th FS, is seen flying in formation with three of her sister ships.

This P-51B, *Hat Jane*, of the 354th FS, 355th FG, shows six aerial victories.

This P-51D, *Chute You're-Faded,* was assigned to the 73rd Tactical Control Squadron 434th Tactical Control Group.

Dee, a P-51D of the 339th FS, is seen flying in formation with three of her sister ships.

An F-51D (s/n 44-74647) at Nellis AFB, Nevada.

The Mustang *Kunk's Klunk*.

The Hellion was attached to the 385th FS, 364th FG.

3PO, an F-6, is seen here at an open house in Dayton, Ohio, in 1945.

Lt. Robert E. Smith of the 75th FS, 23rd FS, piloted this P-51, *Butch*.

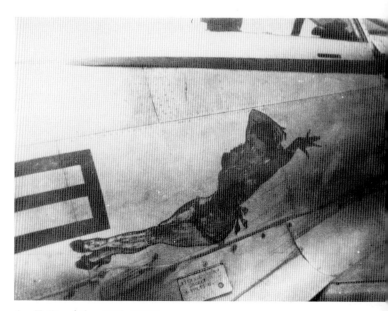

An F-51 of the 18th FBG.

This F-82, *Betty Jo*, flew a record-setting flight from Honolulu to the mainland in 1947.

Note the interesting checkered tail and forward cowling on *Pesky & Larraine*, (s/n 43-12474) of the 59th Tactical Control Squadron, 61st Tactical Control Group.

Stinker was assigned to the 332nd FS.

Janny M. was a P-51D assigned to the 353rd FS.

It is not certain what the significance of *RIT* is, but this otherwise clean Mustang is in transit.

Here is *Round Trip*, one of the first P-51Ds used by the 35th FG. Transition began in early March 1945.

This P-51C, was piloted by Maj. J. C. "Pappy" Herbst of the 76th FS, 23rd FG.

BullDogs, Down For Doubles was a P-51D assigned to the 355th FS. Gordy Graham poses with the 354th FS mascot, Yank.

The Gunfighter, a finely restored P-51D, seen while attached to the Confederate Air Force, clearly exhibits the love and dedication of pilot and owner to machine. Nowadays many

Mustangs make their presence known at air shows across the United States and parts of Canada and the United Kingdom.

The P-51D *Patricia Dean* of the 21st FG is seen on the Island of Guam.

Commanded by Maj. Dean Hess, American pilots, many veterans from Mustang driving in World War II, participated in project Bout One. This operation taught South Korean pilots how to fly the Mustang and in many instances inflicted heavy casualties on North Korean forces. The F-51 pictured in the revetment is Major Hess's ship.

Index